Date: 9/6/22

**PALM BEACH COUNTY
LIBRARY SYSTEM**

**3650 Summit Boulevard
West Palm Beach, FL 33406**

D1772634

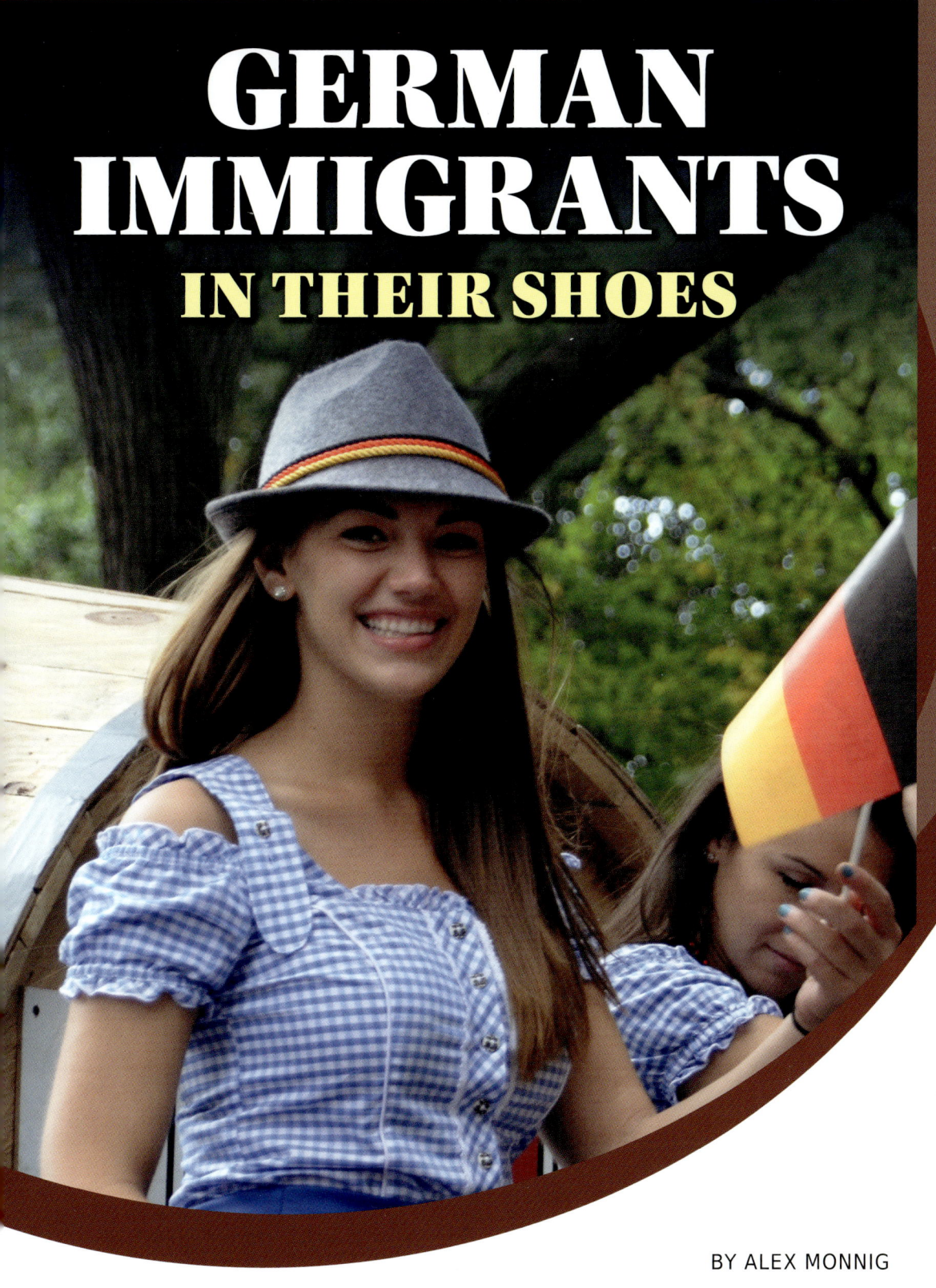

GERMAN IMMIGRANTS
IN THEIR SHOES

BY ALEX MONNIG

Published by The Child's World®
1980 Lookout Drive • Mankato, MN 56003-1705
800-599-READ • www.childsworld.com

Content Consultant: Tobias Brinkmann, Associate Professor of Jewish Studies and History, Penn State University

Photographs ©: Chris Melzer/picture-alliance/dpa/AP Images, cover, 1; Library of Congress, 6; White May/iStockphoto, 9; Daniel M. Silva/Shutterstock Images, 10; Everett Historical/Shutterstock Images, 12, 17, 21, 22; Judith Picciotto/Alamy, 14; Red Line Editorial, 16; Pach Brothers/Library of Congress, 18; Elzbieta Sekowska/Shutterstock Images, 25; Mike Janes/Four Seam Images/AP Images, 26; Bruce Kluckhohn/AP Images, 28

Copyright © 2018 by The Child's World®
All rights reserved. No part of this book may be reproduced or utilized in any form or by any means without written permission from the publisher.

ISBN 9781503820265
LCCN 2016960926

Printed in the United States of America
PA02338

ABOUT THE AUTHOR

Alex Monnig is a freelance journalist from St. Louis, Missouri, who now lives in Sydney, Australia. He graduated with his master's degree from the University of Missouri in 2010. During his career, he has spent time covering sporting events around the world and written more than a dozen children's books.

TABLE OF CONTENTS

Fast Facts and Timeline 4

Chapter 1
The Settlement of Germantown 6

Chapter 2
The Richest Man in America 12

Chapter 3
Fighting for His Country 18

Chapter 4
Finding Answers to Difficult Questions 22

Chapter 5
A German American's Pastime 26

Think About It 29
Glossary 30
Source Notes 31
To Learn More 32
Index 32

FAST FACTS

Important Numbers

- More than two million German immigrants came to the United States between 1820 and 1870.
- Approximately 46 million German Americans live in the United States today.

What German Immigrants Did

- Many of the first Germans who immigrated were farmers and craftspeople.
- Over time, groups of workers formed unions. These groups try to make sure workers are treated fairly.

Where German Immigrants Settled

- New York and Pennsylvania were popular destinations for German immigrants arriving in the 1850s and 1860s.
- Later, many German immigrants moved to the Midwest and settled in states such as Wisconsin, Minnesota, and the Dakotas.

TIMELINE

1683: Germantown, the first German settlement in North America, is **established**.

1776: The United States declares its independence from Great Britain.

1790: Approximately 100,000 Germans have immigrated to the United States by this time, making up 8.6 percent of the country's population.

1846: A hunger crisis hits Germany, causing thousands of Germans to sail to the United States.

1871: Various German states combine to form one nation.

1917: The United States enters World War I (1914–1918), and a massive anti-German propaganda campaign begins.

1945: Allied troops defeat Germany in World War II (1939–1945).

1987: German American Day is established in the United States. On October 6, people honor the effects German immigrants have had on American culture.

Chapter 1

THE SETTLEMENT OF GERMANTOWN

Francis Daniel Pastorius sat aboard the ship *America* on August 20, 1683. Water lapped up against the vessel's sides as it slowly made its way toward land. The ship was heading for the east coast of North America. Pastorius saw land in the distance. He knew it was there that he would help set up a new life for himself and his fellow Germans.

◀ **Francis Daniel Pastorius was born in the German city of Sommerhausen in 1651.**

Pastorius stepped off the *America* onto the shore of Philadelphia, Pennsylvania. In 1683, the United States was not yet a country. But European settlers were setting up towns and cities. Pastorius looked around. He saw opportunity.

Pastorius had a job to do. His first step was to find William Penn, so he set out the next day to do so. Pastorius wanted to set up a safe place for Germans to start new lives. Penn, an Englishman, was one of Pastorius's inspirations. Penn had established the **colony** of Pennsylvania two years earlier, and he called it his Holy Experiment. Penn's goal was to create an area free of religious **oppression**.

"Any good therefore that I can do, or any kindness or abilities that I can show to any fellow creature, let me do it now," Penn said of his experiment.[1]

Pastorius thought of all the possibilities in this new land. He had seen **persecution** firsthand in Germany. Some people were treated poorly because of their religious beliefs. The land in Pennsylvania would be different. It would be a safe place for these Germans.

When Pastorius finally met up with Penn, he was impressed right away. Penn greeted Pastorius with "great joy and love."[2]

Pastorius knew this was the man who could help him. He bought a large chunk of land from Penn. Pastorius also knew that 33 other Germans were traveling to North America from the German city of Krefeld. These families were hoping to escape religious persecution.

The families arrived in Pennsylvania on October 6, 1683. They had spent more than ten weeks aboard the *Concord*. Pastorius had made his own journey only a few months earlier, so he knew how tiring the trip was. The immigrants were not rich and educated like Pastorius was. They were arriving in a foreign land and spoke a foreign language. They were scared.

Pastorius wanted to present a friendly face for the Germans' arrival. He thought back to how kindly Penn had greeted him. So he and Penn decided to greet the Krefeld families.

Pastorius did his best to calm the new arrivals. He wanted them to know they were welcome in Pennsylvania. He and Penn explained their land deal. It was on that October day that Germantown was born.

The new arrivals faced many hardships. They had barely been able to afford the journey to North America. People sometimes referred to Germantown as *Armentown*. This meant "poor town."

William Penn arrived in North America in 1682. He had ▶ established Pennsylvania a year earlier.

▲ Today, Germantown is part of the city of Philadelphia.

Many people looked down on the Germans. They thought the immigrants were not smart because they could not speak English.

But the Krefeld families were ready to deal with problems such as these. They had taken a big risk leaving Germany.

They had done it because they craved religious freedom above all else. They knew returning to Germany's **intolerance** was not an option.

Pastorius knew it, too. So he helped the immigrants adjust to their new lives. The early Germantown settlers included weavers, tailors, carpenters, and shoemakers. They did business with people in nearby Philadelphia.

The Germantown residents were building relationships. It made them feel like they belonged. They were also building a German presence in North America. Over time, that presence grew greatly.

Pastorius in particular became a leading voice in the region. He was one of the first to rally against slavery. He wrote, "There is a saying that we shall do to all men like as we will be done ourselves. . . . But to bring men hither, or to rob and sell them against their will, we stand against."[3]

Pastorius wanted the same thing for all people as he wanted for Germans: freedom from persecution. And Germantown was one of the first places to offer it. It was the start of a strong German influence in what would one day become the United States of America.

Chapter 2

THE RICHEST MAN IN AMERICA

Nineteen-year-old John Jacob Astor set his sights high. The year was 1783. He was selling flutes and other instruments in London, England. The business was going fine. But Astor did not want things to be fine. He wanted to be wealthy.

Astor believed the United States was the place where he was most likely to achieve his dream.

◀ **British general Charles Cornwallis surrendered in 1781, marking a major American victory in the Revolutionary War.**

While in London, he worked hard to learn English. He also learned everything he could about the United States. The new country had declared independence from British rule a few years earlier in 1776. Now that the Revolutionary War (1775–1783) had ended, thousands of Europeans were moving to America. They sensed an opportunity for an improved quality of life.

Astor knew that going overseas was a risk. But he was a risk taker. So, in November 1783, he boarded a ship called the *North Carolina*. All he took was $25 and seven of his flutes. The journey took months, and conditions were cold and miserable. There was little to do, so Astor thought back on his upbringing in Walldorf, Germany. He was raised under the teachings of the Protestant religion. Protestants believed in working hard and living a disciplined life. Astor also thought about his poor father, a butcher who could barely make ends meet. He thought about how he had narrowly avoided getting sucked into the same dead-end life.

Astor had worked hard in school. He had also worked in his father's butcher shop for two years. But after leaving home in 1779, at the age of 16, Astor went to London. Even that journey was difficult. He walked 30 miles (48 km) from his hometown.

▲ Much of the Chesapeake Bay is covered in ice during the coldest parts of winter.

Then he worked on river rafts just to earn enough money for the trip. After arriving in London, Astor worked hard to make and sell flutes. He thought about all he had accomplished. He had made it to London, but he was not going to stop now. Going to the United States was his next challenge.

Astor and the other passengers aboard the *North Carolina* braved the terrible conditions. In January 1784, the ship got stuck in ice for two months. During the wait in the Chesapeake Bay, Astor met a man who had been to America before. The man had made huge amounts of money trading furs. Astor listened closely. He began to realize that his ticket to wealth would be fur, not flutes.

But the ice in the Chesapeake Bay was just the start of his problems. Americans had fought hard to win their independence.

And the British had used German soldiers in the war. As a result, many Americans were suspicious of Germans. Immigrants were sometimes treated poorly. But the immigrants tended to treat each other kindly.

Astor met a shop owner during his first week in Baltimore, Maryland. "We are near countrymen," said the shop owner, who was from Switzerland. "We are glad to see people coming to this country from Europe."[4] The shop owner invited Astor in for a drink. The shop owner and his wife were impressed with Astor. Like many immigrants, they tried to help other newcomers when possible. They decided to let Astor sell his instruments in their shop.

> "They will soon so outnumber us that all the advantages we have will not be able to preserve our language, and even our government will become **precarious**."
>
> —Benjamin Franklin in 1753 on the flow of Germans into North America[5]

Astor sold all of his instruments in three weeks. He used the money to move to New York. Once there, a man named Robert Bowne hired Astor as an assistant in his fur trading company. Bowne taught him how to buy, sell, and prepare furs.

Even when he was exhausted, Astor continued to work hard. He knew this was his big chance.

After a few months, Astor opened his own shop. Then, in 1785, he married Sara Todd, whom he had fallen in love with. She came from a rich family. Her upbringing was the opposite of Astor's. His wife's connections helped Astor meet merchants and traders. They helped him sell furs all over New York. It wasn't long before Astor thought about expanding his business.

GERMAN IMMIGRATION TO THE UNITED STATES

Years	Number of immigrants
1820–1839	130,479
1840–1859	1,361,506
1860–1879	1,475,503
1880–1899	2,024,253
1900–1919	502,949
1920–1939	505,741
1940–1959	696,411
1960–1979	286,758
1980–1999	177,959

▲ **In addition to the fur trade, John Jacob Astor was also involved in real estate in the New York area.**

He began selling to other regions of the United States and even to other countries. The money rolled in.

Astor had grown up poor, and he refused to live that way again. So, he and his wife did not waste their money. They used it to expand their business. Astor spent nearly 50 years in the fur and imports business. He finally sold his **assets** in 1834. When he died in 1848, he was worth an estimated $20 million. The poor German boy had become the richest man in America.

Chapter 3

FIGHTING FOR HIS COUNTRY

Otto Edwin Radke thought he was just like any other kid in Illinois. He had fun with his friends in school. Every day he saw people just like him, playing the same games and going to the same places. But things started to change in 1914. In that year, Germany went to war with several other European countries. World War I was underway.

◀ **Former president Theodore Roosevelt questioned whether German immigrants could be loyal to the United States.**

Otto was a German American. He had been born in the United States, and so had his parents. But his grandparents were from Germany. Many Americans did not want their country to enter the war. They saw Germany as the enemy. That included German Americans such as Otto, even though he had never set foot in Germany.

In 1915, former president Theodore Roosevelt said, "There is not room in this country for hyphenated Americanism. Our allegiance must be purely to the United States."[6] Others felt similarly. Many Americans thought every German might be an enemy spy. Otto saw people acting differently. Kids at school whispered and pointed at him.

The United States entered the war in 1917. President Woodrow Wilson urged Americans to help fight the war at home by staying **vigilant**. He said, "The military masters of Germany . . . filled our unsuspecting communities with vicious spies and conspirators and sought to corrupt the opinion of our people."[7]

Things got worse for Otto and other German Americans. Parts of everyday life were taken away. For example, they could no longer read German-language newspapers. The government had forced the newspapers to print their stories in English.

Many advertisers did not want to be associated with Germans. So, they stopped doing business with German papers. As a result of this lost income, most German papers were forced to shut down.

But newspapers were not the only change Otto noticed. German priests had to speak in English, too. This hurt the communities that met at German churches. Otto's friend's family had even changed their last name to fit in. They switched it from Franz to the more American-sounding Franks.

One day, Otto was walking home from school when he heard two men shouting behind him. They were insulting him. Otto was confused because had not seen the men before. He ignored them, but the insults got louder. He turned and saw the men running toward him. Otto sprinted home. He went in his room and cried.

Otto was a proud American, and he wanted to prove it. So, he enlisted in the U.S. Army even though he was only 16 years old. Otto and his **regiment** set off to fight in France.

Otto boarded a ship next to hundreds of other soldiers. He looked around and saw men and boys who looked just like him. He thought about how they, too, were leaving families and friends they loved to fight against a common enemy.

▲ **Many World War I battles involved soldiers fighting from trenches.**

German troops trapped Otto's group on October 8, 1918. Rain poured on the soldiers. So did toxic gas and enemy gunfire. The soldiers could not sleep. The rain spoiled their food. Otto and his fellow troops tried to hold on. But the weather and enemy attacks were too much. Otto died on October 11, five months after arriving in France.

In the United States, any mother whose son died in battle received an armband with a gold star on it. Otto's mother wore one, just like all the other American mothers who lost sons in the war.

Chapter 4

FINDING ANSWERS TO DIFFICULT QUESTIONS

Gerhard Weinberg couldn't go home. His nose was bleeding, but he didn't want his parents to know. His classmates had beaten him up because he was Jewish. In 1934, these types of beatings happened to Jewish kids all over Germany.

At that time, the Nazi movement was going strong. Nazis hated Jews and treated them horribly.

◄ **Nazis destroyed many Jewish-owned buildings in November 1938.**

Gerhard felt trapped. "You better behave or you'll go to a **concentration camp**," the kids at school told him.[8]

Things continued to get worse. By 1938, Jewish people were not allowed to enter public places such as pools and restaurants. Gerhard was kicked out of school. His parents enrolled him in English classes. One day, Gerhard walked past smoking rubble on his way home. It was the remains of the synagogue that his family attended.

The family moved to the United Kingdom in 1938 to escape the violence. Three years later, they moved to the United States. Gerhard felt more free. He resumed his studies in New York. He no longer got beat up for being Jewish.

After World War II ended, Gerhard Weinberg joined the U.S. Army. His time in the military increased his interest in history. Weinberg could not stop thinking about the Nazis. He knew they were humans like him. So why were they so hateful? And what made them act the way they did? "They're people like other people, which means that other people could fall for this nonsense if they are so inclined," he later said.[9]

These questions stuck with Weinberg. As a result, he dedicated his life to answering them and became a historian.

In 1958, Weinberg made a breakthrough. That year, he was reviewing old German records gathered during World War II. He found an old file that had been mislabeled. Inside was an unpublished book by Adolf Hitler, the Nazi leader. At the time, people thought *Mein Kampf* (My Struggle) was the only book Hitler had written. Now there was a second book.

Weinberg knew the book could help people understand why Hitler did what he did. But publishers were scared. They did not want to print the book, fearing it would spread Nazi beliefs. Even so, Weinberg refused to give up. He knew Hitler's beliefs had started a war that shook the world. He thought the book could prevent another group from acting as the Nazis had.

An English version of the book was finally published in 2003. And Weinberg continued to research the history of Germany.

> "Our citizens of German descent excel in every discipline and open our minds to the expanses of human possibility . . . their unique traditions and customs surround us."
>
> —*President Barack Obama on German American Day, 2009*[10]

His work helped explain the changes Germans have seen in North America since they started immigrating in the late 1600s.

Today, approximately 46 million people living in the United States have German heritage. In 1987, Congress approved the creation of German American Day. It honors the many influences of Germans on everyday American life.

▲ **Adolf Hitler was the leader of Germany from 1934 until his death in 1945.**

Chapter 5

A GERMAN AMERICAN'S PASTIME

Max Kepler's friends gave him puzzled looks whenever he mentioned baseball. Most other kids in Germany loved soccer. They didn't understand why Max played the weird stick-and-ball sport. But Max was determined to make it as a baseball player. He knew he had to go to the sport's home in the United States.

◂ **Max Kepler was only 17 when he played his first minor league game in 2010.**

The Minnesota Twins, a major league team, took note of Max's talent. The Twins offered him a contract in 2009. At the age of 16, Max and his mother moved to Florida. Max would play on a Twins' minor league team to improve his skills. "I wanted to take a risk, give myself a chance," Max said.[11]

The United States was nothing new for Max's mother. She had grown up there, and she moved to Germany to dance ballet in 1984. But living in the United States was totally new for Max. He missed his friends back in Germany. While they were enjoying their teenage years, Max was in a foreign country.

Max had never seen pitchers throw so hard. Most pitchers in Germany couldn't throw faster than 80 miles per hour (129 km/h). But in his first year in the United States, Max saw pitchers throw nearly 100 miles per hour (161 km/h).

Max attended a school that was across the street from where he played. His mother came every day to watch him. "I don't think I would have gotten as far in baseball without (my mom), because she's the one who pushed me to go abroad," Max said.[12]

Max went to school every morning. Then he rode his bike across the street to the practice field. He did his homework while riding the bus to games.

27

▲ **Max circles the bases after a home run.**

As a player, Max showed that he was a speedy outfielder. He steadily rose through the minor leagues. In 2015, he was named Most Valuable Player of the Southern League.

Later that year, he finally got the call. He was going to play for the Twins. Max made his major league debut in September at the Twins' home field in Minneapolis, Minnesota. The team's mascot helped him feel at home with a sign that said "Willkommen Max." In German, it meant "Welcome Max."

Max still missed some things about Germany. In particular, he missed his friends and German cooking. But he had found success in the United States. He was becoming a star in America's most beloved game.

THINK ABOUT IT

- Why do you think many immigrants were willing to leave part of their family in Germany when they moved to the United States? What would you have done if you were in their situation?
- How would the United States be different if millions of Germans had not immigrated to the country?
- Why do you think some Americans treated German immigrants poorly during World War I and World War II?

GLOSSARY

assets (AS-ets): Assets are things that people own. John Jacob Astor had many valuable assets that he sold before dying.

colony (KAH-luh-nee): A colony is a territory that is settled by people from another country and is controlled by that country. William Penn established the colony of Pennsylvania.

concentration camp (kon-sin-TRAY-shun KAMP): A concentration camp is a prison-like area that holds people whom a government opposes. Millions of people died in Auschwitz, the largest concentration camp of World War II.

established (uh-STAB-lishd): Established means officially started. The colony of Pennsylvania was established in 1681.

intolerance (in-TOL-ur-uns): Intolerance is the act of not accepting somebody else's beliefs or behavior. Many Germans immigrated to the United States to escape religious intolerance.

oppression (uh-PRESH-uhn): Oppression is the unfair and cruel use of power to stop somebody from doing something. Francis Daniel Pastorius wanted to help Germans who had faced religious oppression.

persecution (pur-si-KYOO-shuhn): Persecution is the harassment or unfair treatment of people because of their beliefs. Many Germans came to the United States to escape persecution.

precarious (pri-KAYR-ee-us): Precarious means dangerous or uncertain. Benjamin Franklin thought the U.S. government would be precarious if too many Germans immigrated.

regiment (REH-juh-munt): A regiment is a large group of soldiers. Otto Edwin Radke's regiment fought in France during World War I.

vigilant (VIJ-uh-lunt): Vigilant means watchful or alert. During World War I, Americans were encouraged to be vigilant and look for German spies.

SOURCE NOTES

1. "Quotations from William Penn." *ushistory.org*. Independence Hall Association, n.d. Web. 7 Nov. 2016.

2. William J. Buck. *William Penn in America*. Philadelphia, PA, 1888. 130. *Google Books*. Web. 7 Nov. 2016.

3. "Francis Daniel Pastorius, Germantown Renaissance Man, Arrives in Philadelphia." *Philly.com*. Philadelphia Media Network (Digital), LLC, 6 Aug. 2013. Web. 7 Nov. 2016.

4. "John Jacob Astor Quotes." *Quotewise.com*. Quotewise.com, n.d. Web. 7 Nov. 2016.

5. Cristina Costantini. "Fear of Immigrants Is as Old as America Itself." *ABC News*. ABC News Internet Ventures, 14 May 2013. Web. 7. Nov. 2016.

6. Mary J. Manning. "Being German, Being American." *Prologue* 46.2 (2014): 16. *National Archives*. Web. 7 Nov. 2016.

7. "The WWI Home Front: War Hysteria & the Persecution of German-Americans." *Authentic History Center*. AuthenticHistory.com, n.d. Web. 7 Nov. 2016.

8. Daniel Gross. "As a Kid, He Fled Nazi Germany. As an Adult, He Found Hitler's Forgotten Second Book." *PRI*. Public Radio International, 1 Jan. 2016. Web. 7 Nov. 2016.

9. Katie Eastman. "Historian Escaped Nazi Germany and Became 'Hitler's Editor.'" *Warner Cable News*. Charter Communications, 10 Jan. 2016. Web. 7 Nov. 2016.

10. Pamela Engel and Gus Lubin. "Here's Why There Are So Many German-Americans in the US." *Business Insider*. Allure Media, 7 Oct. 2013. Web. 7 Nov. 2016.

11. Phil Miller. "How Did Soccer-Loving Max Kepler from Germany End Up a Twin?" *StarTribune*. StarTribune, 15 Aug. 2016. Web. 14 Dec. 2016.

12. Jim Caple. "How Twins OF Prospect Max Kepler Journeyed from Germany to Majors." *ESPN*. ESPN Internet Ventures, 19 Apr. 2016. Web. 14 Dec. 2016.

TO LEARN MORE

Books

Demuth, Patricia Brennan. *What Was Ellis Island?* New York, NY: Grosset & Dunlap, 2014.

Flatt, Lizann. *Immigration*. New York, NY: Crabtree Publishing, 2015.

Roza, Greg. *Immigration and Migration*. New York, NY: Gareth Stevens Publishing, 2011.

Web Sites

Visit our Web site for links about German immigrants: childsworld.com/links

Note to Parents, Teachers, and Librarians: We routinely verify our Web links to make sure they are safe and active sites. So encourage your readers to check them out!

INDEX

Astor, John Jacob, 12–17
Baltimore, Maryland, 15
Bowne, Robert, 15
Chesapeake Bay, 14
German American Day, 25
Germantown, Pennsylvania, 8, 11
Hitler, Adolf, 24

Kepler, Max, 26–29
Krefeld, Germany, 8, 10
London, England, 12–14
Mein Kampf, 24
Minnesota Twins, 27, 29
Nazis, 22–24
oppression, 7
Pastorius, Francis Daniel, 6–8, 11
Penn, William, 7–8

Philadelphia, Pennsylvania, 7, 11
Radke, Otto Edwin, 18–21
Revolutionary War, 13
Roosevelt, Theodore, 19
Walldorf, Germany, 13
Weinberg, Gerhard, 22–24
Wilson, Woodrow, 19
World War I, 18
World War II, 23–24